The Little Gullah Geechee Book

THE LITTLE GULLAH GEECHEE BOOK
A GUIDE FOR THE *COME YA*

DR. JESSICA BERRY

TABLE OF CONTENTS

Foreword
Introduction

FOREWORD

I'm not sure if there has been any research done on the subject, but I'm 100% sure that coffee shops are one of the best places to meet random people for the first time. The vibe is always chill and the smell of freshly brewed coffee beans lulls you into a space of congeniality.

The free wi-fi keeps you huddled over your laptop, shoulders hunched, typing away to the beat of a caffeine-induced drum. The low hum of Kamasi Washington's saxophone playing in the background puts you in a good mood whether you realize it or not.

Not to mention, good coffee shops are always filled with people. And places filled with caffeinated people, with access to free wi-fi and deadlines to meet, ensure that people are on their best behavior. Do anything crazy and the whole act would be livestreamed, tweeted, Snapchatted, and BlimBlammed[1] before the perpetrator left the parking lot.

Which is why Jessica's decision to meet me in a Summerville area coffee shop, two years ago, was a great decision. Not only did we strike up a genuine friendship, but it showed her ability to think 10 steps ahead, a skill needed when trying to push an envelope that many have seen, but

---

[1] I literally just made that up. But it sounds like an actual social media platform, right?

very few have tried to advance with any
authority.

It was in that coffee shop that we discovered
how much we had in common. From our shared
connection with South Carolina State
University[2] to our burning desire to see our
beloved language and dialect recognized for
what it is: an act of ingenuity and genius.

The Africans who were enslaved, ripped
from their homeland, shipped, tortured,
brutalized, and forced into labor were people.
Humans. Mothers. Fathers. Brothers. Sisters. And
these humans had their own languages, their
own traditions and norms. They had names.

[2] Home of the Mighty Bulldogs and the Marching
101!

Memories. Plans for next week. Plans for next month.

And while I do not know many details about them, I know for a fact that they did not arrive in America with an ability to speak English. Many of them didn't speak the same language even when they were in their respective West African homelands. Throughout that mental, emotional, and physical trauma, they found a way to survive. Shoot, they did more than survive, they invented. By taking pieces of their respective languages, traditions, and customs and mixing that with the language of the Buckra, my ancestors created a delicious stew of a culture, now known as Gullah Geechee.

Everyone loves shrimp, grits, rice, and sweetgrass baskets now. However, that hasn't always been the case. A stigma has followed the practitioners of Gullah Geechee culture since it came into fruition. Charleston is one of the few places in the world where a native, speaking in native tongue and practicing native traditions, are frequently ostracized. Have a sharp dialect in New York City and you can still become Mayor. Have a syrupy Southern drawl in Alabama and you can still become the Governor. Sound Gullah Geechee in Charleston and prepare to be presumed unintelligent. Treated as less than.

Have your public school system attempt to fix your speech via ESOL[3].

Despite public pressure, dirty looks, or inquiries about their intelligence, there have always been people who are proud to showcase the totality of Gullah Geechee culture. However, it must be noted that in the last few years, there has certainly been a surge in putting that pride on display.

With the rapid growth of the Charleston Metro Area[4] (28 people moving to and 8 being born a day), there is a feverish movement by

[3]Charleston schools consider Gullah language barrier: http://bit.ly/GullahBarrierCCSD
[4]https://www.crda.org/news/2019-exactly-how-many-people-move-into-the-charleston-region-each-day/

natives to secure the cultural and intellectual property of the Gullah Geechee people. We seek to own our culture in ways that respect the foundation our forefathers and foremothers laid before us, while keeping eyes squarely on the future.

People like Chef BJ Dennis who educates consumers on the connection between Gullah Geechee cuisine and other cultures within the African Diaspora.

People like Akua Page and Chris Cato of the Geechee Experience who use millennial-centric techniques like podcasts, memes, and YouTube videos to educate, entertain, and empower Gullah Geechee people.

People like Gullah Griot Sara Makeba Daise who is building on the storytelling legacy of her parents, creators of the television show Gullah Gullah Island, to spread a message of positivity and pride for Gullah Geechee culture.

People like Trelani Michelle, the author of Krak Teet: A Catalog of Savannah's Black-in-the-Day Biographies which highlights the experiences of native Gullah Geechee elders from 1920 to 1970.

People like Sunn m'Cheaux, founder of GullaTeacha.com and the first Gullah professor to be hired at Harvard's renowned African Language Program.

People like Queen Quet, and her Gullah /Geechee Nation organization, who are leading advocacy efforts for Environmental Justice on Gullah Geechee land.

People like me, the founder of Red Rice Day in Charleston, South Carolina and Charleston Sticks Together, a brand that presents an uplifting view of Gullah Geechee culture through streetwear influenced merchandise.

And of course through people like Dr. Jessica Berry, the author of this book, who has spent the bulk of her professional experience trying to impress upon the uninitiated the academic merits of studying Gullah Geechee language and culture.

I'd like to think that our conversation, in that Summerville coffee shop, sparked the idea for her to create this book. And that by her creating this book, and your subsequent decision to read it, she is bringing much needed awareness to the oldest American-born culture.

By no means is this book going to explain the entirety of the culture, rather, consider this your entry level course into Gullah Geechee. May it provide a spark in you to learn more and increase your respect for both our ancestors and those who carry the banner present day.

KJ KEARNEY

A native of North Charleston, KJ is a product of Charleston County public schools and a proud 2005 graduate of South Carolina State University.

A 2015 recipient of the Summerville Councilman's Award for his work in the community, KJ has also served as a columnist for the Charleston City Paper where he routinely wrote about economic disparity, race inequality, social injustices, and hip-hop culture. His writing earned him two nominations for the

AAN Awards, which highlights the best alt-news writing in the US and Canada.

KJ wrote the proclamation for the creation of "Red Rice Day," which was officially acknowledged, by the City of Charleston on Saturday September 29, 2018. "Red Rice Day" was created by KJ to honor the traditional Gullah Geechee dish and its West African precursor Jollof.

He is also the founder of Charleston Sticks Together, which presents an uplifting view of Gullah Geechee culture, one of the oldest American born cultures to have ever existed.

Find him on Twitter and Instagram at @KJBeenya.

Visit   www.CharlestonSticksTogether.com to purchase his Gullah Geechee inspired merchandise.

INTRODUCTION

I am so glad that you have either decided to visit the beautiful Lowcountry or are considering your next trip. You made the right decision by spending time in this beautiful place that has so much to offer.

Also, you are pretty smart for picking up this little book that will provide some valuable information about the Gullah Geechee people and the treasure that they hold on their tongues. Whether you are a *tourist* traveling through the Lowcountry corridor, a *come ya* who has made the Lowcountry your new home, or a *been ya* who was born and raised under the moss of the beautiful oak trees, there is always something to learn about Gullah Geechee.

To The Tourist

Perhaps you are a tourist visiting the Gullah Geechee corridor for the first time eager to learn more about all that the Lowcountry has to offer. Something special drew you to the beautiful Southeastern coast of the United States.

It could have been the delightful weather, historic charm, or alluring beaches. Whatever enticed you to come here, brought you to the right place where you are sure to encounter the Gullah Geechee people.

Your ears will hear the melodic rhythm of a language unknown to many. You may not know what Gullah Geechee sounds like, but when you question if the Black people that you see are from Jamaica, 99% of the time they are not; They are Gullah Geechee.

This quick read will enlighten you about the language that you will hear or hear about as you navigate the tours, stores, and restaurants in the area.

The Come Ya and The Teacher

Charleston and surrounding areas are one of the fastest-growing in the United States. I always meet *"come yas"* who relocated to the area for work or play. They love the scenery, the food, and the proximity to the ocean.

I've met *come yas* from across the country, particularly from the North and Midwest. Each of them brings their own cultural diversity to the existent distinct Lowcountry culture. Most have little knowledge that Gullah Geechee exists and are intrigued from afar.

Interestingly, many of the *come yas* are educators. New graduates who are eager to enjoy the Charleston scenery and teach the youth of the Lowcountry. As you can imagine, many teachers who *come ya* are unaware of the cultural and linguistic differences that they will encounter when they walk into their classrooms.

While this is not meant to be a comprehensive or in-depth presentation of the Gullah Geechee history, culture or language, it is a seed. A seed that will undoubtedly bloom, after continued study, into appreciation of this unique US culture; a culture and language that isn't going anywhere.

To The Been Ya
You *been ya* and you know exactly what it means to be Gullah Geechee. This book is for you. This book is in celebration of all of the things that make you unique. It is homage to the sacrifices made, the community built, the plans to preserve what we know to be a gift to this world.

I hope that as you read this book, you learn at least one new thing, find joy in seeing the places that you have been, and experience excitement when you read the words and phrases that so easily roll off of your tongue. You are Gullah Geechee and you should be proud. #ForeverGeechee

*** In a later chapter, I will cover some Gullah Geechee grammar. This image is a fun display of some of the most common Gullah Geechee grammar.

Chapter 1

GULLAH GEECHEE: HISTORY

The history books do not tell the story about the development of Gullah Geechee. What we know about the development of Gullah Geechee, is what has been passed down orally through generations of Gullah Geechee descendants. Although the complete history is not included in the textbooks, it is rich and has shaped Black culture, as we know it in America today.

The 15th century was an interesting time in world history. New nations were developing while others were thriving. The second-largest continent, Africa was home to kings, queens, doctors, lawyers, dentists, farmers, merchants, and midwives, although they may not have had those modern titles at that time.

Most importantly, there were people who lived and had established lives, homes, and families. They enjoyed the simplicity and beauty of life. They had plans for having and raising children, plans for going to family gatherings, plans for what to do on the weekend with friends, and plans not to be stolen and forced into a life of servitude.

They used their vast knowledge of the land to provide for their families and those closest to them. I was not there to see all that they had planned and accomplished, but I can only imagine the dreams deferred.

The United States was officially formed and like all start up businesses the need for money became increasingly apparent. European settlers and leaders realized the need to establish infrastructure and economy. I will not speculate on exactly how the conversations went or whose idea it was to begin slavery, but those conversations changed my ancestors' lives and the course of history.

The Transatlantic Slave Trade was the largest, most complex, global transport and sale of humans recorded in history. Large ships were taken across the Atlantic Ocean from North America and Europe to Africa. While there, thousands of African people were shackled and transported on long and dangerous journeys to North America. They were systematically separated from their tribes and from their families.

In an effort to decrease the enslaved African's ability to communicate with one another, they were strategically separated from their families and friends who spoke the same languages. Many of the enslaved spoke various African languages that were not mutually exclusive.

During this journey, the enslaved were shackled together and forced to lie down shoulder-to-shoulder underneath the boats. This was done in an effort to transport as many people as possible in one trip. As one can imagine, the conditions were not sanitary or humane. During the "Middle Passage" many suffered from illnesses, while others chose to take their own lives during the journey.

This journey was one of survival and endurance for the Africans who were inhumanely torn away from their lives and families. During the journey, new relationships were formed as people who were not related by blood supported one another like family. These harrowing trips and the relationships that were formed were the catalysts for social arrangements on the plantations.

Upon arrival in the US, historians agree that approximately 40% of the enslaved Africans were brought to the city of Charleston, South Carolina to be sold[5]. They were dispersed to the various plantations in the United States to work as free laborers and property of their owners.

Many of the enslaved were placed on plantations along the coast stretching from North Carolina, South Carolina, Georgia, and Florida. This coastal region is currently known as the Gullah Geechee Cultural Heritage

[5]National Park Service. Lowcountry Gullah Culture Special Resource Study and Final Environmental Impact Statement. Atlanta, GA: NPS Southeast Regional Office, 2005.

Corridor[6]. It was along this corridor, on islands like Wadmalaw, James Island, St. Helena Island, and inland areas like Awendaw, Wando, and Huger that the Gullah Geechee language was born.

Enslaved Africans were responsible for the daily running of the plantation from the house to the fields. Communication may have been difficult among them as they were now separated from their families and tribes and placed with others who looked like them, but did not speak the same language. Additionally, many were required to work in the plantation

[6] https://gullahgeecheecorridor.org/ Gullah Geechee Cultural Heritage Corridor Commission

home, but were not able to speak the English of their owners.

The need for communication for buying and selling is the typical catalyst for the formation of a Pidgin language variety. In the case of Gullah Geechee the enslaved, borrowed some English grammar and mixed it with the vocabulary of African languages like Mende, Hinto, Yoruba, and Krio creating a pidgin variety that was only used for communication.

This new common language (Pidgin) was taught to children becoming their first and only language (i.e. Creole) in place of the African languages of their caregivers or English of their owners. The newly formed English-based

Creole is what we know today as the Gullah Geechee language.

While we do not know exactly how the name Gullah Geechee came to be the name of the language, there are several theories and connections that have been made based on the African tribes that were represented in the corridor region. The name Gullah potentially derived from the *Gola* people of Angola while Geechee is thought to be from the *Gidzi* people of Sierra Leone.

Other geographical distinctions are those who live near the Ogeechee River in Georgia are referred to as Geechee while those who reside on the South Carolina Sea Islands, identify as only Gullah or the combined Gullah Geechee.

Regardless of the in-group distinctions, the Gullah Geechee people are unified in the language and culture created by their ancestors, as evidence of the African life, culture, and language that they were forced to leave behind.

Chapter 2

GULLAH GEECHEE CULTURE

Surrounded by the greater Charleston and Lowcountry culture, the Gullah Geechee culture is distinct and unique. I never quite valued the uniqueness of the culture until I ventured off to college and met people who did not do the little things like crabbing and fishing on the weekend, attending crab cracks, or going to a watch night service on New Year's Eve.

It was interesting to me that the things that I found so familiar were unfamiliar and exciting to others. Truthfully, it made me appreciate all of the things that are Gullah Geechee. It made me proud of my culture and all of the things that we hold dear. There are a few things that are heavily valued in the Gullah Geechee culture: family, religion, and food.

CULTURAL
WAYS

WHILE TOURISTS get to see and purchase the beautiful sweetgrass baskets that are a trademark of the Gullah Geechee culture, those baskets are a reflection of family, which is at the center of what makes the Gullah Geechee culture distinct. The making of the Sweetgrass basket is not a craft that is executed by all Gullah Geechee people.

Certain families within the community have intentionally kept the basket making tradition alive by teaching the skill to the next generation. In particular, this trade is most frequently passed down in families from Mt. Pleasant, South Carolina and smaller surrounding areas like Awendaw, Tibwin, Cainhoy, and islands like

Johns and James Island. If you take a trip down Highway 17, you will see little wooden huts on the sides of the road. Those huts are sweetgrass basket huts, owned by local Gullah Geechee basket makers.

Before the abundant commercial and residential development, it was common to see the elders enjoying a breezy Saturday morning making baskets and talking to friends and family on the side of the road. Each basket is meticulously handcrafted, with great attention to detail. Passersby and tourists often stop to admire and purchase baskets to adorn their homes.

The sweetgrass basket's original purpose was agricultural. The sweetgrass basket is a tangible retention of African heritage that is unique to the Gullah Geechee people. I can only imagine that in many ways creating the baskets was a pleasant reminder of home for the enslaved. The sweetgrass basket has since become a trademark of the culture. So, when you see the beautiful baskets for sale in the Lowcountry, know that they are a labor of love, shared by family, to be treasured, respected, and enjoyed.

Other local treasures include the rod iron gates created by local artisan and master blacksmith, Phillip Simmons. Since his passing, Philip Simmons Elementary, Middle, and High have been erected in his honor. His home and work shed is now a museum [7] in his honor,

---

[7] http://www.philipsimmons.us/aboutsimmons.html

remembrance, and preservation of his artistic skills. He was most notably known for his rod iron fences that still adorn the million dollar homes in Downtown Charleston. Gullah paintings by Jonathan Green provide vibrant imagery that captures the true essence of Gullah Geechee people and culture. His work can be found in Lowcountry art museums and in the Charleston Market.

In recent years, there has been a surge of storytellers, crafters, artisans, and performers who showcase their traditional Gullah Geechee cultural skills as a way to secure the continued vitality of the culture.

RELIGIOUS
WAYS

THE SWEETGRASS baskets reminded the enslaved of the safety of their homeland and in the same way, the local church provides comforting gathering places for Gullah Geechee people. The church is where families gather to pray for and with one another. The church also serves as a space for community meetings and planning to occur.

In Gullah Geechee churches, you can still hear the distinct double clapping, foot-stomping African inspired rhythmic percussion beats. The call and response style songs are reminiscent of the melodies sung along the African coast. Attending a church service with Gullah Geechee people is sure to be an experience. Do not be surprised if a person breaks out in a shouting dance while a group of ushers encircle them as they praise God.

The *ring shout* is a tradition of the Gullah Geechee people that continues in churches across the corridor. Gullah Geechee people believe in having faith and hope to endure. The local church is a microcosm of the culture and refueling station for faith and hope that is often diminished by life's burdens.

In an effort to maintain contact and communication with members some small rural churches continue to have "class leaders" who are responsible for a group of people within the church. Historically, these classes were created to ensure that important messages would be shared among the people. The class leaders were responsible for all of their class members being made aware of the news.

Another significant event in Gullah culture is that many churches gather on New Year's Eve to host *watch night services*. The original watch night service was a time when the enslaved gathered at the "praise house"(i.e. church) to hear the news of the Emancipation Proclamation becoming law, which symbolized their freedom from slavery[8]. However, when I was growing up,

---

[8] The African American Desk Reference Schomburg Center for Research in Black Culture Copyright 1999 The Stonesong Press Inc. and The New York Public Library, John Wiley & Sons, Inc. Pub. ISBN 0-471-23924-

these services were only explained as a time to gather with church, family, and friends, to pray in the New Year. During these services, a designated watchman (typically a longstanding male church member) calls to another male across the sanctuary for the time.

With all of the lights turned off, through the darkness, flashlights shine on a clock so that all of the congregants know exactly how many minutes remain until the new year is ushered in. Church members are on their knees "praying in the new year" and petitioning God for His covering and blessings over the new year that is approaching.

Some churches also use this time to call out the names of family members who passed away during the year. A reminder to those in the room that life is precious and the opportunity to be alive should be valued. Once the clock strikes midnight, the church erupts in celebration of God carrying them safely into another year. The celebration ends with songs, hugs, and tears of joy.

Churches in the Gullah Geechee culture are extensions of family-a larger community of folks that are responsible for one another regardless of kinship. The Gullah Geechee people understand that it takes a village to maintain the community. For example, attendance at vacation bible school, church, choir rehearsal, and Girl Scout meetings are times when parents are not present with their children.

While in other cultures this alone time would signal an opportunity for children to engage in bad behavior, Gullah Geechee children know that they should maintain their best behavior. In the Gullah Geechee community, it is understood that the adults who are present have full permission to discipline the children in the same way as their parents would.

The children also know that discipline will not only come from their "community parent," but that they would be disciplined again by their real parents when they reach home. Discipline isn't the only area where our "community parents" are engaged. In fact, they encourage, support, pray, and sow into the lives of the youth, like their parents. As a result, Gullah Geechee

children receive money, sweets, hugs, and
unlimited support from community parents
when significant achievements are obtained.

FOOD
WAYS

❧

GULLAH GEECHEE food traditions are treasured and passed down in the community. Traditionally, Gullah Geechee people lived off of the land by producing crops like rice, okra, and sweet potatoes. In particular, rice is a staple dish of the culture that is typically eaten with every meal--every single meal! Specifically, *Red Rice* is a signature dish that is similar to the popular West African *Jollof* Rice.

Gullah Geechee people have kept the Red Rice recipe and passed it down for generations. Red rice can be found served at various restaurants along the corridor and is typically adorned with bell peppers, onions, bacon and

Roger Wood sausage for flavor and always with a side of fresh fried fish, shrimp or chicken.

Okra is a signature vegetable of the Gullah Geechee culture. Gullah Geechee people created *okra soup,* which is similar in some ways to Louisiana seafood gumbo. This hearty dish is served over white rice and is made with okra, corn, tomatoes, neck bones, and shrimp.

Some people even add butter beans and green beans to their soup. One thing that is special about the Gullah Geechee way of cooking is that each family has a unique way of preparing each dish so that no two plates will taste the same. The consumption of seafood is not just a pastime, it is a lifestyle of the Gullah Geechee people.

Due to the close proximity and easy access to the Lowcountry waterways, the Gullah Geechee diet is heavily reliant on seafood. Shrimp, fish, blue crabs, and oysters are the superstar seafood dishes of the culture. On the weekends, you can find Gullah Geechee people gathered together with friends at a *crab crack* or an *oyster roast.* These are special gatherings where Gullah Geechee people sit around a table and eat the seafood that was caught that day.

Along with the seafood, you may also find a large pot of *Frogmore Stew* simmering for the guests. Frogmore Stew is a Lowcountry classic also known as Beaufort stew, which includes blue crab, shrimp, corn, potatoes, sausage, onions and other spices and an occasional egg for good measure.

The Gullah Geechee people are creative and resilient. They were able to hold on to more African traditions and language than any other African American culture in the US. Thus making them distinct from any other African American group across the country.

The Gullah Geechee people have held on to African language, culture, and food traditions that have disappeared from general African American culture in the US. Their ability to retain much of their African identity was due in part to their isolation from mainstream culture. The islands and many rural inland areas, like

Huger, were only accessible by boat until the 1920s.

Additionally, diseases carried by mosquitoes were deadly to the plantation owners, which encouraged them to leave the enslaved along on the plantations during the warm months when mosquitoes would be plentiful. Similar environmental conditions along the US coast to the African Coast allowed the enslaved to develop natural immunities to many of the diseases that would kill their keepers.

These unexpected circumstances created ideal conditions for the enslaved to maintain important and recognizable characteristics of their African identity.

Chapter 3

GULLAH GEECHEE LANGUAGE

The Gullah Geechee language is a United States treasure. Linguists recognize Gullah Geechee as the only English-based creole language spoken in the United States. A Creole language is an oral language system resulting from the mixing of two distinct languages. Creole's are derived when individuals who speak various languages are in close contact.

However, the way that the two languages come in contact is not always the same.

In the case of Gullah Geechee, the close proximity of the different languages that was not due to voluntary, or routine exchanges of goods and services but was a means of survival for the enslaved. This initial mixing creates a pidgin that is taught to children and become their first and only language. When the pidgin becomes the first language of the next generation it has fully emerged as a creole language.

Creole languages have consistent, rule-governed grammar and a stable vocabulary. For Gullah Geechee, English is the dominant language that contributes most heavily its vocabulary and grammatical structure. Various

African languages like Yoruba, Igbo, Efik, and Mende, Gola and Gidzi influence to the unique vocabulary, grammar, prosody (rhythm), and intonation (pitch) of the language[9].

One frequently asked question is, "What's the difference between Gullah and Geechee?" The short answer is that there is no difference. However, there are some subtle distinctions as it relates to language structure (i.e. grammar) and vocabulary. The Gullah Geechee people are one people, with one language, and culture. Sociolinguists have documented some regional and generational segmentation that make distinctions between the two words.

---

[9] See Lorenzo Down Turner's seminal 1949 text, *Africanisms in the Gullah Language*

Most frequently noted are regional delineations where those who live on the Sea Islands of South Carolina and Georgia (i.e. Sapelo Island, Wadmalaw, St. Helena) self-identify as Gullah while those who live inland (i.e. Huger, Awendaw, Mt. Pleasant) identify as Geechee. Additionally, some natives also refer to themselves as *Saltwater Geechee*.

The generational segmentation explanation of the terms Gullah Geechee is often used by the millennial generation (circa 1981-1996) whom refer to their use of the language as Geechee due to the decreased use of African vocabulary and increased use of English vocabulary but with Gullah Geechee intonation, pitch, and inflection.

I am included in the millennial generation who believe that my grandmother's generation (1900-1960) spoke a more authentic Gullah due to the heavy presence of African vocabulary that is not as much a part of the Gullah Geechee vernacular my peers and I use. The Gullah Geechee of my grandmother's generation, would be highly unintelligible to non-natives compared to the variety that is spoken by millennials.

Gullah Geechee originated out of a need for enslaved Africans, who were intentionally separated from their families and tribes, to communicate with one another and with their owners. The enslaved Africans were left unattended by their owners for long periods of time due to extreme environmental conditions, which could cause severe illness and even death for their owners.

The isolation allowed the enslaved to retain many of their African traditions, food, music, vocabulary, and language. The maintenance of African traditions in Gullah Geechee distinguishes it from African American culture across the United States.

Popular opinion is that the Gullah Geechee language is dead or dying, but locals strongly disagree. Gullah Geechee is a communal language where members of the community only speak the language with other natives. When they are not around other speakers, they code-switch to a more Mainstream English variety. In other words, you would have to be a part of the community to hear the language.

Additionally, Gullah Geechee has been passed down orally and there is no standardized written form. These factors combined may lead outsiders to believe that the language is dying. The opposite is true as the language and culture is thriving in Gullah Geechee communities as evidenced by children continuing to learn it as their first language.

In the past, Gullah Geechee people have been skeptical of outside interest in their language and culture. However, with each new generation a new level of pride is emerging and celebrating Gullah Geechee publicly.

Gullah Geechee Grammar

The grammatical structure of the Gullah Geechee language distinguishes it from Mainstream English, African American English, Southern White English and every other type of English dialect that is spoken in the US. When people hear Gullah Geechee they know that they are hearing a distinct language but may not be able to fully explain the differences that are heard.

These differences are so distinct that natives who do not know one another can typically pick out other Gullah Geechee speakers even if they are attempting to code-switch to a more Mainstream variety.

For example, on the campus of South Carolina State University, a fraternity called

Chuck Phi Chuck was created as a unifying group for Gullah Geechee college students. Students recognized that something was different about their language and culture and in response created a fraternity, which acted as a micro Gullah Geechee community on campus.

Chuck Phi Chuck was an extension of the Gullah Geechee community and students found solace in knowing that there were others around who understood the legitimacy of their native language. The creation of Chuck Phi Chuck fraternity is a modern example of how the Gullah Geechee people value community and wherever they are, they connect with other natives who truly understand who they are and more importantly what they say.

No matter the language a person speaks, the words that are used are important. In this section I share some of the most common grammatical structures in the Gullah Geechee language. Several of the vocabulary words in modern Gullah Geechee are English, however, the tone, rhythm and pitch in which they are used, create the recognizable melodic sound of the Gullah Geechee language.

Gullah Geechee is markedly different from Mainstream English in all aspects of language, including speech sound production and vocabulary, with the most notable differences documented in the distinct grammatical patterns.

These grammatical features, coupled with the unmistakable rhythm and pitch have caused unfamiliar listeners to consider that Gullah Geechee is "broken English". However, consistent and rule-governed use of certain grammar structures, strategic placement of words and phrases, and an undeniable tone and rhythm provide a guide for what is permissible in the language.

Not unlike other non-mainstream varieties like African American English, a lot of what is said in Gullah Geechee is not based on the differences in the words that are used but more on the context of the conversation. Gullah Geechee does not have a written form, but the language system is stable, systematic, and rule governed. For instance, let's take a look at the infamous *universal pronoun*.

The Universal Pronoun

The term *universal pronoun* is not an official linguistic term, but it represents how the Gullah Geechee people use this traditional creole form. This is one of the most distinguishable features of the language. No matter what part of the corridor a Gullah Geechee person resides, when they use E (also written as *e, ee, Ee*) as a signal of in-group affiliation.

Not long ago, during one of my lectures, an undergraduate student asked, *"Why do those Charleston people always say e instead of he or she?"* This was a fun moment during the class because she was not the only one who was curious about how Gullah Geechee people use their language.

They all wanted to know and so my response went something like this:

In Mainstream English, the pronouns *He*, *She*, and *It* make the distinction between masculine (i.e., He), feminine (i.e., She), and neutral (i.e. it) gender pronouns. Unlike English, Gullah Geechee does not make a distinction between these gender pronouns. Instead, Gullah Geechee uses the universal creole pronoun, *E*. Gullah Geechee people do not have to distinguish if it is *He*, *She*, and *It*.

Most often it will be the context of the conversation or some gesture that will indicate who or what the *E* is of the conversation. According to Turner (1949), this grammar pattern resembles the non-gender specific pronoun usage in West African languages such as Igo and Yoruba.

Gullah Geechee	English Gloss
E ova day.	He/She/It is over there.
My daddy, *e* gone home.	My daddy, he went home

So, when you ask a Gullah Geechee native for directions to your hotel, do not be surprised if they respond, *E down da road da way*! (It's down the road, that way.) You asked about the hotel so the hotel is now *E*.

Substituted Forms
In the Gullah Geechee language, there are several grammatical forms that can be deleted or

substituted for another form in a sentence. While contemporary linguistic work talks about these forms as being absent, I like to consider these forms substituted. Categorizing these grammar forms as being absent implies a negative connotation.

When we think of someone or something as being absent, it makes us believe that it should be there, but it is not. For example, when I take roll in my courses and someone is not there that should be they are considered absent. Since we know that Gullah Geechee is a Creole language, it is important that we change our thoughts regarding the grammatical structure of the language from that of nonconformity to Standard English rules (i.e. absent forms) to

Gullah Geechee speakers applying and using the grammatical rules of the Gullah Geechee Creole language (i.e unnecessary).

In other words, we do not need to use all of the proper English words to say what we mean. The grammatical forms that are required in English are not required in Gullah Geechee. We can use fewer words and still communicate what we mean. In the following examples, I refer to these forms as substituted because they can be interchanged for the standard form when a Gullah Geechee speaker chooses to code-switch to Mainstream English.

With that in mind, let's take a look at some of the most common substituted forms in the Gullah Geechee language.

PRONOUN IT

The pronoun *it* can be substituted with *e* or *um*.

Examples:

Gullah Geechee	English Gloss
She kick *um* hard.	She kicked *it* hard.
e been hard.	It was hard.

Possessive Pronoun (His, Hers, Its)

Possessive pronouns are substituted with *e* or used in conjunction with the word *she* depending on the context.

Examples:

Gullah Geechee	English Gloss
E burn e lip.	It hurt **its** lip. He burned *his* lip. She burned *her* lip.
She can buy she own.	She can buy **her** own.

Possessive Word Form

In English, possession or ownership is indicated by the apostrophe + s being added to a noun. In Gullah Geechee language ownership is implied by the context and not by the addition of the apostrophe + s.

Gullah Geechee	Mainstream English
Das my momma car.	That's my mother's car.

Tense and Agreement

The Gullah Geechee language does not have a formal indication of tense. This pattern is common in West African languages like Ewe, Yoruba, and Mandinka. What this means is that in Mainstream English, tense is marked using *–ed* (i.e Walked), *–s* (i.e. balls), *–ing* (i.e. Walking), and *am*; while in Gullah Geechee, these forms do not have to be used.

Tense is often indicated by the context of the conversation or is indicated by the use of a word like yesterday (past), or today (present), tomorrow (future). The following example shows how Gullah Geechee speakers use tense markers in reference to calling someone.

Examples:

Gullah Geechee	Mainstream English
I call um. (tenseless)	I call him/her/them. (tenseless)
She (e, he) da call um.	She call**s** him/her/then.
I callin um I da call um.	**I am** call***ing*** him/her/them.
I call um, yesterday. I been call um.	I call***ed*** him/her/them.
I beena call um.	I have been call***ing*** them.
I done call um.	I have call***ed*** them
I been done call um.	I had call***ed*** them some time ago.

Some scholars believe that the Gullah Geechee language never acquired *-ed* as a marker of past tense. Even irregular past tense is not marked in the language, which makes for an interesting conversation with unfamiliar listeners.

As with many other languages, assimilation to modern mainstream language practices has heavily influenced the increasingly frequent inclusion of regular and irregular past tense in the Gullah Geechee language.

Gullah Geechee	English Gloss
Regular Past Tense e jump clean cross da gate.	He/she/it jump*ed* across the gate.
Irregular Past Tense e *fall* off a ladda las week.	He/She **fell** off of the ladder last week.

Chapter 4

GEECHEE DOWN TA DA SOCKS

High school was a fun time[10]! I remember when the song *Y'all boy look ya*[11] came out and it was (and in my opinion remains) the Geechee anthem. We were proud to finally have a song that captured the essence of who we were. Also popular during that time was the phrase, *I Geechee down ta da*

---

[10] Circa 2000-2004. I'm getting old.
[11] https://www.youtube.com/watch?v=aHX8I2AfOI8

socks! This one is a favorite of mine because it finally gave us a phrase that demonstrated pride in our culture and who we were.

Out of these songs, young, millennial Gullah Geechee voices emerged. This marked the beginning of a generation proud to be called Geechee. This generation would not allow the negativity that was once associated with the term Gullah Geechee define who they were; they were Geechee and proud.

So in that spirit, presented below are some Gullah Geechee words and phrases. One caveat is that although the Bible's New Testament has been translated into Gullah Geechee, the language remains an oral language with no standard written variety. Therefore, when the language is written, speakers interpret the words based on how they hear or desire to spell them.

I try to stick with some of the spelling conventions that are common in certain publications, but I write the words how I hear them and use them in personal conversation. This feels more authentic to me and I hope will capture the essence of how language changes and is expressed by different speakers.

This is not an exhaustive list, but some of the most common phrases (and in some instances not so common phrases) that I heard growing up that you may hear by locals in conversation.

Table 1: The People

Gullah Geechee	English Gloss
Come ya	A person who is not originally from the Gullah Geechee corridor but migrated to and made a home in the region.
Been ya	A Gullah Geechee native
Buckra or Buckruh	White (Caucasion) person
Churn or Chillin	Children
Tita or Tituh	Sister
Bubba	Brother
Gal	Girl
Dem	Them
Hunnuh How hunnuh fa do?	You 'How are you doing?'

I'll always remember my mother getting upset when we would say, "Dem *churn* beena ack up daday!" She would tell us that you "churn" butter and those were children. We would laugh and continue to use the word churn, just not around her.

Tituh was my grandmother's nickname and *Bubba* was my uncle's nickname; Or so I thought! It wasn't until I began studying the Gullah Geechee language that I learned that both the words Tituh and Bubba had origins in West African languages.

You may remember Binya Binya Pollywog from the show Gullah Gullah Island[12]. His name was not an accident as it described the fact that he was native and had lived on Gullah Gullah Island for a long time. So is the same for the Gullah Geechee people. We identify as *Been ya* because we are natives, we speak the language and live the culture and it distinguishes us from those who are new to the corridor, the ones who just *come ya*.

---

[12] Nickelodeon children's television series from 1994-1998

Table 2: Animals, Food, and Other Common Things

Gullah Geechee	English Gloss
Fush	Fish
Cudda	Turtle
Nab	Crackers
Skrimp	Shrimp
Yam	Sweet Potato
Māda	Tomato
Wegatuble	Vegetable
Boonkie E big bookie	Buttocks 'He/she/it has a big buttocks'
Zink	Sink
Frigidare	Refrigerator

―――――

When I read the *Tortoise and the Hare* in kindergarten, my little brain could not reconcile the names that they were calling these animals to the names that we called them at home. When my aunt sent a plate home for dinner it was rabbit and when my grandmother made a stew it was cudda stew (not tortoise or turtle stew). I figured it out eventually, but man was that confusing.

―――――

In the Gullah Geechee language, we substitute the short *i* (i.e. *it*) sound for the *u* (i.e. put) sound in several words. One of the most recognizable and commonly used words is *fush*. So when the native waiter takes your order and they ask you if you want the fresh *fush* of the day, you'll know that is the freshest fish you have ever eaten, likely caught by some Gullah Geechee *fush*amen (i.e. fishermen).

I'd hear my granny use the words *wegatuble, zink, and frigadare* very often. I'm not sure that these words are used frequently in public, but in Gullah Geechee homes and community they are still used by the elders.

———

Boonkie was a forbidden word in my house, but that did not mean that we wouldn't use it. This is easily one of the most common Gullah Geechee words that is used by past and present generations of speakers. To have a large *boonkie* in the African American community is a good thing, so do not be surprised if you hear this word while out and about in the Lowcountry. Oh, and if you think that the person is talking about you, do not be offended as it's probably a compliment.

Table 3: Common Words

Gullah Geechee	English Gloss
Bussin Dem crab been bussin!	Really good 'Those crabs were really good!'
Skrate	Straight
Skreet	Street
Fa	for
Rink E rink boonkie	Stink (smells like urine) 'He/she is stink.'
Cu'red Cu'red da boy tall!	Wow! 'Wow, that boy is tall!'
Innit You ga go, innit?	Right 'You are going to go, right?'

Fresh	A person who is promiscuous
Shree	Three
Yeddi You yeddi wha I say?	To hear 'Did you hear what I said?'
Mine I mine churn	To babysit (typically children) 'I babysit children'
Dareckley I ga be de dareckly	In a moment or soon I'm going to be there in a moment (soon).

When you taste true Gullah Geechee cooking,the best way to describe it is that it's *bussin*. The red rice with sausage or okra soup with fresh shrimp is sure to be *bussin* if a native made it.

———

The *-sk* substitution for *-st* in *skrate* and *skreet* are commonly used not only in Gullah Geechee, but in African American English. Do not be alarmed or think down on the drive-thru attendant when she asks you if you want a *skraw*. This is a normal and well known sound substitution in the Gullah Geechee language.

If you have the opportunity to speak with a Gullah Geechee native, they may be able to tell right away that you are a *come ya*. They can tell by your accent or because you may be asking them for suggestions on things to do, places to visit and eat. Do not be surprised when they say, " You'een from roun here, innit?" *Innit* is our way of confirming that what we are saying is right or wrong. So in this instance, your response should be, "Yes, you're right, I'm not from here. I'm from [*Insert city here.*]

Table 4: Common Phrases I

Gullah Geechee	English Gloss
E 'E gone."	He/She or it (The universal pronoun) He/She/It is gone.
Beenga I beenga do um.	Was going to I was going to do it
Ga	Going to
Gone now!	Quit! or Stop! or Go away!
Up da winda	Put the window up
Down da winda	Put the window down

As you may have noticed in the previous tables and in the grammar section, many Gullah Geechee words and phrases carry multiple meanings. When you are conversing with Gullah Geechee speakers pay close attention to the context of the conversation as it will typically alert you to which meaning of the word or phrase is intended.

True story: When I lived in Louisiana, I made a new friend at church who would allow me to ride with her to choir rehearsals and church events. As you know, Louisiana Summers are brutally hot. I recall riding with her early one Sunday morning and it wasn't quite warm enough for the air conditioning to be turned on, so I asked here to *down the winda*. The look she gave me was one of utter confusion. I repeated my request and she responded, "I have no idea what you mean!" I had to think of another way to ask and finally said, "Please put the window down." It took a little while to think of how to translate my request into Mainstream English but once I did, we had a good laugh all the way to the church.

———

I *beenga* write this book years ago, but somehow I never got to it. In other words, I had plans to write this book a long time ago but life got in the way. However, I'm glad that it is finally done and whoever *ga* read it will enjoy learning about this language and culture.

Table 5: Common Phrases II

Gullah Geechee	English Gloss
Pee up Da boy pee up in class.	To wet your pants 'That boy wet his pants in class'
Mash-up e mash up mout.	Pouting 'He/She is pouting or frowning.'
Eat up E eat up head.	Messed up 'He/she has messed up hair.'
Shed up!	Shut up!

Fool up	1. Crazy person 2. You don't associate with someone
Da one dey fool up. I don't fool up with em.	'That person is crazy' 'I don't get along with that person'
Head bad or Bad head da one dey head bad!	To have some mental health issues 'That person is crazy'

In the Gullah Geechee language the word *up,* does not mean that something is going up. It is typically used as an intensifier, added to a single word to intensify its meaning. So, the addition of the word *up* would translate to mean *very* or *really*. I remember *up* being added to several words and used as an insult while riding on the school bus. Some examples include: dumb up (really dumb), fat up (thick in a good way; or really fat). Another use for the term is the phrase *e big up* meaning that a female is pregnant.

———

School teachers, especially those in the preschool and elementary grades, who teach Gullah Geechee children should expect to hear the popular phrase, "Johnny pee up!" quite often when students wet their pants.

Mental health is an extremely important topic in society today, particularly in the African American community where we do not speak openly about our struggles with mental health. In the Gullah Geechee language, the way we describe someone who may have some mental health issues is with the phrases *fool up* or *head bad/ bad head*. Both phrases share a similar meaning and many times they are used jokingly when describing someone whose behavior or actions are out of control.

Table 6: Common Phrases III

Gullah Geechee	English Gloss
een H'een/She'een ga do um.	Am/is not 'He/she's not going to do it'
I'een/He'een/She'een know.	I/He/She don't/doesn't know
Who dat?	Who is that?
I ga box you in yo mout	To hit or fight (punch) someone 'I'm going to punch you in your mouth'
Look ya!	Look! or Come here
Hear say I hear say e leave home.	To hear gossip or news 'I heard that he left

	home'
Take sick e take sick in da church.	To become ill 'He/she became ill while in church.'

When you hear the words, *I ga box you in yo mout* it's time to make your exit. These are fighting words and an indication that things are probably not going to go well. Other times, this is the threat that Gullah Geechee people use in order to inform someone that they are not happy and should back off.

Use of the phrase *who dat* in Gullah Geechee is not the same as the New Orleans slogan famously associated with the Saints football team. In the Gullah Geechee language *who dat?* is a true question of *Who is that?*

When I was younger, I remember going in to the local community store and an elder asked me, *"Who pa you?"* I had no idea what he meant, but he kept asking. Eventually, I realized that he was asking me who my father was. I haven't heard that phrase used in years, but it's always stuck with me as a Gullah Geechee phrase of the older generation.

Table 7: Common Phrases IV

Gullah Geechee	English Gloss
Da Hag da hag beena ride me las night.	A spirit that sits a person while they sleep. 'The hag sat on me last night.'
Root	Witchcraft

———

For some, the Gullah Geechee people are associated with practicing witchcraft. Although there are rumors and stories of those who practiced or were affected by such practices, it is not common for Gullah Geechee people to have conversations openly about the practice. These are the hidden conversations that you will not likely hear while exploring the town.

Table 8: Common Phrases V

Gullah Geechee	English Gloss & Example
Wha ya want?	What do you want?
Man shoot!	Aww man!
Good evlin.	Good evening.
Get from roun ya	Get away from here.

———

As people pour into the church for the evening program, it's common that older Gullah Geechee speakers will not say, "Hi," but will instead greet you with a pleasant, *Good evlin.*

———

If a student does not want to complete work that a teacher assigned, if a person does not want to comply with a request, or if someone messes up on a task that they are completing, their Gullah Geechee response will not be "Oh no" but *Man Shoot*! Sometimes we add an extra man on the end for emphasis even if the person that we are speaking to is female (i.e. man shoot man!). We also insert a teeth suck before we begin the phrase *man shoot man*. This is customary and is not meant as a sign of disrespect. The teeth suck adds emphasis to the phrase and quite frankly, the phrase would feel incomplete without it.

Table 9: Uncommon phrases but my momma used to say these!

Gullah Geechee	English Gloss
Kiddy by da door.	That's it, I'm done with you.
New broom sweep clean.	Someone is taking over and will make changes.
Lil pitcha got big ears.	Little children hear a lot.

Poorly hope.	The person is going to die.
Scape det.	Escaped death.
E take sick.	He/She got/became sick

———

As a sign of respect, Gullah Geechee children are not allowed to be in the room or in the midst of adult conversation. The Gullah Geechee saying *lil pitcha got big ears* is an expression that is used to remind adults in the room that children are present and that they should monitor what is being said.

If you are around Gullah Geechee families, then take note of the fact that children are typically excused while adults are conversing. They are also typically seated at a separate table, in a separate room during dinner, so that they do not participate in or over hear adult conversation.

Chapter 5

DO'S AND DON'TS

There are always some things that you do not do when you visit friends or family – like put your feet on their couch! The same is true for your visit to the Lowcountry. There are many DOs and important DON'Ts for you to know so that you do not get *box off* (i.e. punched in the mouth). We want you to enjoy your time in the Lowcountry so pay special attention to and enjoy these suggestions.

Celebrate Gullah Geechee

Gullah Geechee is likely one of the most unique languages you will hear in the coastal regions of the United States. It is rare, but pleasant to the ear. Its melodic rhythm captivates unfamiliar listeners and inspires conversation.

Gullah Geechee people want others to be excited about learning more about the culture and language. Most Gullah Geechee people enjoy speaking about our history and the traditions that have been maintained for centuries.

To celebrate Gullah Geechee is to tell someone about it who may have never heard of its existence. Celebrations are big deals. Gullah Geechee is a big deal. So celebrate knowing that reading this book, learning about this culture and language can inspire others to do the same.

Honesty, who wouldn't want to celebrate a beautiful and positive remnant of a dark time in American history. Gullah Geechee is a bright spot on that dark blemish called slavery because it embodies the resiliency of people who survived and created a culture that honors their African heritage.

Don't Say That Gullah Geechee Is Broken English

To say that something is broken is to imply that it needs to be fixed. The Gullah Geechee language is not broken English because the rules that govern its use have been cemented in history and on the tongues of natives.

Although the grammatical rules of the language do not match mainstream rules, when Gullah Geechee people speak to one another they share an understanding of what has been said. After having read this book, you can now describe the Gullah Geechee language appropriately not as broken English or a dialect but as an English-based Creole language spoken along the Eastern coast from North Carolina to Florida.

Buy A Palmetto Rose Or
Sweetgrass Basket From Local Artisans

One of the Gullah Geechee people's most treasured traditions is the making of sweetgrass baskets and palmetto roses. Sweetgrass baskets were originally agricultural tools used by the enslaved on the plantations to complete various tasks. They were not decoration, but rather a necessity for their way of life.

Presently, the sweetgrass basket is an artisan commodity that is used as decor for the *come ya* and as a reminder for the *been ya* of the importance of preserving the culture. Be sure to buy a palmetto from the young Gullah Geechee men and sweetgrass baskets in support of the hard work of local artisans like Jennifaye Singleton of *GeecheeGal Baskets* and Geraldine Dawson. These beautiful handmade crafts are one-of-a- kind keepsakes to remember your trip to the Lowcountry.

Don't Ask A Gullah Geechee Person To, "Say Something In Gullah" Or "Speak Gullah"

Resist the urge to ask someone to speak Gullah Geechee. Some speakers will oblige your request, while others may not have nice words to share with regards to your request. For so long, the Gullah Geechee language has been treated as a second rate, broken English.

In response, the Gullah Geechee people tend to reserve using the language freely only when they are in the company of other Gullah Geechee people. When they are around *come yas*, they to code-switch to a Mainstream English variety to fit into the modern culture.

Don't Make A Gullah Geechee Mad
But Get Us Excited

I know, I know, this sounds crazy. Hear me out -- There are two occasions when you are guaranteed to hear a native switch into full-blown Gullah Geechee. These occasions are when we are upset or when we get very excited. When you make a Gullah Geechee person upset, be ready to hear all of the Gullah Geechee language that you can handle.

On the flipside, when we get excited (i.e. when someone tells us that the are bringing us some blue crabs) we are not concerned about code-switching and allow our Gullah Geechee to roll off of our tongue in celebration.

Don't Ask If Gullah Geechee People Are From Jamaica

We are not Jamaican, although we love our Caribbean family. History is clear that many of our ancestor's relatives ended up being enslaved on the Caribbean islands. The Gullah Geechee language has island flair, as it was born on the Sea Islands of the South Carolina and Georgia coasts. Additionally, history tells us that enslaved Africans from the same regions traced to the Gullah Geechee people were also transported to several Caribbean islands.

As a result, our languages share some common vocabulary, prosody (rhythm), and linguistic structure. Resist the urge to ask if a Gullah Geechee person is from Jamaica. Instead, enjoy the melodic words that fill the air when you hear them speak.

Visit Special Places Along The Corridor

I remember Saturday family day trips downtown to walk King Street, ending our day at *The Pineapple*. Back then we could swim in the large pineapple fountain but that tradition is no longer allowed. We would play in the water fountain at the *Waterfront* and race to get a swing after a long day of fun (side note: the swings are always taken).

You could catch us on the *Battery* walking by the ocean or sitting under the white gazebo, eating *Chilli Bears* (i.e. frozen kool aid with fruit), on a hot summer day.

Field trips to the museum, Patriot's Point, and Charlestown landing came to be elementary school expectations. As children, we enjoyed getting away from the humdrum of regular school days in Huger to explore what Charleston had to offer. When we crossed over the Mark Clark (i.e. I526) the air smelled like rotten eggs from the paper mill, we knew that we were on our way to a day of adventure.

After you have explored some of the places discussed above, be sure to carve out some time in your schedule to explore local places like the Avery Research Center for African American History and Culture, consider participating in Gullah Tours, the Gullah Museum in Georgetown, the Gullah Geechee Visitor Center in Beaufort, The Penn Center on St. Helena Island, and Brookgreen Gardens in Murrells Inlet and the magical Angel Oak Tree on John's Island.

Grab Something Good To Eat

As you've read, food is an important part of the Gullah Geechee Culture. We enjoy a good plate of food; especially seafood.

Here are a few good places to visit to taste some Gullah Geechee cooking: Nana's Seafood-Soul, Nigel's Good Food (Try the Geechee wings), VIP Bistro, My Three Sons of Charleston, Carolima's Lowcountry Cuisine, Gillie's Seafood, Hannibal's, Bertha's Kitchen, and Buckshot's Restaurant.

This list will give you a head start on some amazing Gullah Geechee restaurants to enjoy while you visit the coast.

Eat Blue Crabs, Oysters
And Other Fresh Seafood

We love our seafood down here in the Gullah Geechee corridor. It's a way of life to eat food fresh out of the ocean on a regular basis. As a visitor you should oblige and be sure to make your way to Ravenel Seafood, Marvin's Seafood (i.e. Starvin' Marvin) and Charlie Brown Seafood for some fresh seafood like Oysters, Clams, fish, fried, steamed and garlic Blue Crabs.

Consider Ways That You Can Embrace The Gullah Geechee Culture And Language
    BUT...
Do Not Engage In Gullah Geechee Cultural Appropriation

As mentioned in the Foreword, the Gullah Geechee people are actively fighting to maintain the authenticity and ownership of the language and culture.

In recent years, we have seen *come yas*, inappropriately adopted some cultural customs, practices, and ideas for monetary gain. Misrepresentation of cultural traditions by those who are not Gullah Geechee, diminishes the work that is being done by natives.

Chapter 6

FOREVER GEECHEE

There is a new banner being waived all across the Gullah Geechee corridor. It is a banner of pride in a culture that has existed for hundreds of years. Social media has created a platform for Gullah Geechee millennials to begin writing the language as a way to communicate with others in the community.

This is an important shift in the preservation of a traditionally oral language. Additionally, the creation of memes on Instagram that educate others on the culture have re-energized native pride in Gullah Geechee language.

As we move forward and as the landscape changes across the corridor with new construction and new people, it is imperative that those who speak the language acknowledge, embrace, celebrate, and fight for its continued use. One way that this will be accomplished is by parents passing down the language and traditions to their children just like the generations before them.

As natives disperse across the nation from the West to the East coast, Gullah Geechee is who they are. New development is happening quickly, subsequently encouraging mass in-migration to the Lowcountry area. In response, Gullah Geechee people continue to rally with preservation efforts in relationship, cultural practices, land retention, and language.

Like all languages, the Gullah Geechee language is changing. New words and phrases are emerging and some are fading as the generations pass on. However, even with the change in vocabulary, the heart of the Gullah Geechee language and people remain the same. Our hearts remember the journey that our ancestors took. We acknowledge and remember the unprecedented trials that they had to endure, and the beautiful gift of a Creole language that they left behind.

I encourage you to take some time to research and learn more in depth about the history of the Gullah Geechee people. Do not be afraid to speak to the locals while you are in town. We are happy to share with you the best local restaurants and places to go to have an authentic Gullah Geechee experience. It is because of our ancestors' journey, that we get to speak this beautiful language.

This book is an active disclaimer that the negative stigma associated with being Gullah Geechee is no more. It is our time to be Gullah Geechee and proud. So in the spirit of celebration of efforts to preserve the culture, language, and history of Gullah Geechee join us as we proclaim, *Forever Geechee.*

ABOUT THE AUTHOR

DR. JESSICA BERRY is a Gullah Geechee native of Huger, South Carolina. She is a nationally certified speech-language pathologist.

She completed her Bachelors' degree at Winthrop University and her Master's degree at South Carolina State University in Speech Pathology and Audiology. Her doctoral studies were completed at Louisiana State University in Communication Disorders with a minor in Linguistics and focused child language with emphasis on the grammar of children with Gullah Geechee heritage.

Dr. Berry is a university professor, researcher, and child language expert who enjoys educating others about modern Gullah Geechee culture and language. Inspired by her experiences as a Gullah Geechee speaker navigating complex and negative classroom experiences, she has devoted her career to advocating for the recognition, celebration, and inclusion of Gullah Geechee in mainstream culture. Dr. Berry's favorite saying is, *"Gullah Geechee been ya, een gwine nowhere."*

Her research interests include child language development and disorders in the context of regional dialect variation, non-mainstream English grammar, and non-biased assessment. She is currently an assistant professor of speech pathology and audiology at South

Carolina State University where she teaches undergraduate and graduate research and language, and literacy courses.

Dr. Berry is passionate about the Gullah Geechee language and has worked as a translator/transcriber with the Smithsonian Museum of African-American History and Culture project. She has provided professional development seminars, and webinars for over 500 educators in South Carolina and Louisiana.

Dr. Berry is an experienced presenter having presented at numerous local, regional, and national conferences like the Inaugural International Gullah Geechee and African Diaspora Conference and the American Speech-

Language Hearing Association National Convention.

Dr. Berry is a wife and mother of two beautiful daughters. In her free time, she enjoys traveling, reading, and singing.

CONTACT DR. BERRY

———

Follow on Instagram
@Iamjessicaberry or @thegeecheescholar

Twitter
@iamjessicaberry

Email
Jberrycollective@gmail.com

Made in United States
Orlando, FL
20 February 2023